God Inspired Poetry
By
Ann Wright

PUBLISHED by PARABLES
Earthly Stories with a Heavenly Meaning

God Inspired Poetry
Ann Wright

Published By Parables
August, 2020

All Rights Reserved. No part of this book may be reproduced or utilized in any form or by any means, electronic or mechanical, including photocopying, recording, or by any information storage and retrieval system, without permission in writing from the author.

    ISBN 978-1-951497-82-8
    Printed in the United States of America

Readers should be aware that Internet Web sites offered as citations and/or sources for further information may have been changed or disappeared between the time this was written and the time it is read.

God Inspired Poetry
By
Ann Wright

PUBLISHED by PARABLES
Earthly Stories with a Heavenly Meaning

A Dream"

A flabbergasted night ship upon a kintly harrow
Gone wander array
Gone wandering away
An understood song
A juxtaposed meadow of melody long
An invitation unspent
His hindrance unclempt
A happier place where dreams you want are true
A heaven so new
Yet, God's blessings so big ignoring none
His heart vastly deep with comprehension

Ann Wright

"In a Name"

His hand lifted my soul in His Palm
My light spoke
My heart filled
My eye never wander again
My hands abreath
My sky always seen
Just a justice ring
    Amen from the bell that promise spoke
Like an angel sung
Like a wind blew
My heart loved Him
Him whose name is Jesus
A name above them all

"Peace-making"

One has the inventive variable
One has the cease fire
One has the extinguisher and the other well,
Sparkly shoes that I know are frictioning a fight
But when joe pushes buttons I never notice the shoes
His line sung every time, a hollowed out tune
And the pause amid the sparkled shoe a tension
for those inventive enough to bring just a butter knife
When shotguns are never necessary
A thin line between inspiration and tension
The Price of Peace must he heard!
Sparkly shoes though

Ann Wright

"Amen"

Upon the likening sight
Upon that unwritten, write
She sang a song of twilight not night
Unwalking like summer sun spent
Her moon a turned a summer sent
Yearly wander through understood song
A flower regrown
Under walked a Man knew her tune

In light we spin
In light we walk
Like a twilight wonder in a hallowed out clock
Her time not short
Her gown anew
Like a lover in a twilight hue
Happy are they as happy are we
Hourly flowers filled the soul of her might
Her mind aright
Her faith a spark
Her spark enough to light a candle in the dark

"Holy Ghost"

A shed no tear
A cry no sigh
For mourn will come to dry thine eye
A hush a bye
A hush a cry
And who a mourn I sighed to thine eye?
Jesus's Ghost to fix a sigh

Ann Wright

"When to Cry"

A boy
A cross barren he writes
Unlike that majesty once told he wept barrenly like a child in the night
But my soul not afixed
My heart not set right
But a cry again
A cry a north
A cry again because
I lost

"We Won"

Unlooked at that pectar is schism
A petal upon a night cloud
A sprinkler sown
A water yet known
A summer hath grown
His Love always known

Ann Wright

"A Cross"

This cross, more like a kite as a magnet it pulls
And a smile once slain
Reborn into truth
A Savior's Love greater than a love of any other
He brings no request
He brings no fear

"For my Soul"

Glowing on the triumph a tune my soul can sing
His heart a greater depth
To swim
Green
Unlike a sea
A yours guarding my life
An angel's name
A glimmer brighter than hope
A love shining hut
Among the trees a spacious view
Amid my savior's domain
A cove secluded my mind free
A guiding light from a book
A greater light within

His face that shone
And still shines
-thank God for Christ

Ann Wright

"Unspoken"

A yonder sky bitten by a fluffy cloud anew

His fluff a sea
His fluff mastered
His scent captured
Is placing conceived
It's force received

Juxtaposed
Jehovah's work
Perfected
Unspoken

The Lamb

"Frailty?"

A wholehearted harmony of peaceful pilgrims are we
Wet take delight in our family
Although, take may be more like receive.
Our hearts prevail through sanity
No walls only light need be
Our faith prevails through frailty

Ann Wright

"Race?"

A twilight race of humans
A twilit night
Nightly 'pon the candle we speak
Candled hands
Handled iced glares
When the temperature was too warm

"A Request"

A brozen flower
With power to match the dawn we bring
Glad tidings

Flowers in the breeze died about 1000 years ago to a tempter sow written

But we see a brazen flower amidst a cold breeze

A wedding

A joker played a trump card spoken when their words became few
When their words he knew what they were talkin' 'bout
That sad note when
The flowers die
"None taken"
—amen

Ann Wright

"Loyalty"

Upon a walking midnight
A storm which crept by it's ease
Never attuned my fault to thy stormy shore
Upon the midnight eve a walk I went
I returned with my savior at hand
No tomorrow aturned
Just a justice ring
From the bell that promise spoke
Upon a walking midnight

"Amid"

Justice is spoken on the tristeps of our humanity unspoken
A world yet written
A world yet understood
Of the haphazard coming to life like the trihazardous commotion

Ann Wright

"All Things"

In the trip try southern time
In that mountainous sky
My heart leapt
As Jesus in the womb
Upon Elizabeth's speak
A hallowed night
A covered wing strewn
His words better than any other
I claim no glory
I claim no pride

In a spinning bowl of truth
A golden cup of our dna rests
Unlike chemistry
More life blind Love
We know His truth
And God makes all things possible

"Or Just sleep"

Upon a ship last seen that midnight sailor a strewn
His eye captive and told
His slumber a night once strew
The waves did pile
The wind did blew
A grapp'ed open in the twilight sky seen
The hundred fifty miles between
Finding that light on a water askew
A friend another friend placed their minds a new
When His Might wake came down
A glass lake new
A glass lake knew

Ann Wright

"Power, —thank God it's not for sale"

Brandished blues matchless black and turning flowers back to their proper time
When the mad hatter seems much to sane

Purposely misspelled we walk
A band of misfits are we

Walking our walk to the light only the Dawn brings
Prayer helps more than modesty today
For the sunset claims it's own hour
Believe it or set

Tumulted twixt tween
The Blood drips my toes
To be drank
No vampires here
Guess I'll go dig a hole somewhere else

I could use some dream playdough
Priceless solds! Unheard of sales!
A fright, "gasp!"
A cold Ghost to tell
Holy yet though
Thank God it's not for sale
Man versus power; power versus man

"The Power of the Blood"

The potpourri fond of it's day clim'ed and saw where the gold in righteousness spoke.
Amid that brokers joke
"Who gotta say I'm broke?"
"Who gotta say I'm broke?"

Now that who be gone
Now that
Now that
We can sing
If hallelujah we can sing!

In that place where only His name is spoken
Everyday conversation lacks existence
Everything said is just His Name spoken in love
All flows perfectly and all know when to fall
How peculiar one must wonder
But not even say, inflection-like contextual conversations bloom
Because all that is said is His name in love

Ann Wright

"Visibility"

Giving light a patron gets spoke
Of Good News dreaming in the air
Light a scent it plays with my dance
Like a friend I never and always knew
His heart greater than my own
It won my fail swept sigh

A glass house I did not break
A bent reed He did not break

His hands pierced
His heart shone
Visibility became from it

In His name we speak

"Green Hope"

The fiddle playing the needlepoint scissors
All aglow like a juxtaposed banter of midnight spoken
A new page broken and untried
A new life strewn about a comforter's delight
By the gotten green hope
His triumph spoken throughout the sky
Thank God we're on His side
Verily, I say to you
One need-
Understand the Prince of Peace

Ann Wright

"Son"

Upon a wandering night
A shallow once wrought
A silence with brought a clocking page a turn
His eyes a glow
None like the savior I know
A taint of continued mire
A guttering quallow upon the guessing morrow
A verily turn within a shadow
A sense not made
A change hath stirred
Hatchling of sunshine behind her ear where most sun won't shine
Unlike sin more like blood
Upon her written said "son"

"His name was Match"

Unwritten smiles rough top like a match
But it's smell unique
Like a match once knew
But if it were about who we knew
It must be Jesus we know
A page now written like the smile that matches the match

Ann Wright

" What to Do About Pain "

Is the pain real
And if it were would it go away?
And if it wasn't would it stay?
My remedies gone
My medicine a joke
Just blends the lines
Looking for a way out, I apply pain to the wound
Stretching for that good reason
But is it treason?
They say I'm not alone but maybe alone in pain is better.
I don't want to share this meal with anyone for it tastes of medicine
But is it treason?

"Hold Onto Home"

Hold onto home
Because your falling out of it
Your mind races new thoughts slowly to an open wound of conclusion

Hold onto home
Because God was there
Yet not
As a mystery yet to eat, no devour, in His presence
Whether dark or stormy
Light or smiling but
laughing
Which revealed a bright haunt full of love and hope

Hold onto home
Because there is love there
Invisible in nature
Possibly in the small
Or in the teeth cracked or straight

Hold onto home
All the fights and misgivings suspicions and hugs
Because all were clean and how lucky are you to have them
Tire them up in memory boxes sharing to the needed few
For some ate nothing and their lips dry for your drink

I said, hold onto home because your falling out of it

Ann Wright

"All"

all tribes
all languages
all nations
all peoples

    A wide circle
    A multitude

    Seeing smiles instead of color
  Seeing feeling of heart instead of state
   Seeing faith instead of
language
And faith as The language

"The Other Cheek "

I have no screws!
I threw them all in the floor!
Violently!, so they bounced back with a thud and hit me in the shin!

Unfortunately, someone or something picked them up and put them all in a bucket.
Picked them up invisibly with my back turned to sell on the street to anyone who could use them in evil judgement on some unsuspecting soul.

But at least I have no screws

Ann Wright

"Water"
It was water
With you
Not a fire

But a numbness gone
A flood
A glow
Fullness of heart

With a smile
Grasping the wind I fight
When I only want more
Did I know happiness before you?

I tie you around my neck
Around my finger
Around my ankle
In my words and thoughts those heard and silent

"Description of self "

Beauty from God
Wearing my favorite tennis shoes
Nail polish add something to do
Army coat hating all war
A cross around my neck
Forcing a smile
A poet
Lonely yet loved
"Is it real?"
Coconut oil and handmade perfume
She cooks
Collecting stamps of approval
Smart and wise
Naive
Complicated yet simple

Ann Wright

"A boy?"

One day, a very sad boy asked a stirring question.

"Do you have a mom or a mother?"

I knew what he meant right away and contemplated how it applies to my life for days

I agree I have both a strong strict mother and a warm caring mom. I knew her as mommy, now mom but we call it Mother's Day

But he argued, "A mother is mean and only mean he says with evil eye and all!"

I understood and felt a deep grief in my heart and throat
    I began to appreciate my mom even more

She's strong when there is no strength
She's the humility where they're should be pride
She's the warmth in cold
She's more to me than a "mother"

"Everybody thinks they're a good dancer"

First of David danced
But my mom's dance
    Silly set best
My dad's dance
    Ridiculous at best
My sisters dance
    More of a modern grove probably my favorite of the lot but clearly not enough
"My " dance
Extrodinary! Uplifting! Energetic! In step and perfectly on beat with the music the beat one with me the lyrics in my head up and out to God my toes in step with my feet fingers lit up with my hands it's fire! It's water!! It's Me! It's my dance! Not theirs. Everybody thinks they're a good dancer

"Snakes "

More than cold
More at a temperature no one can fathom
Can't tell if it's too hot or too cold?!

Just try to give your grace
Just try to give you forgiveness
Just try and give your peace
Just try and give your lessons
Just try and call it out!
Just try and leave!
Never helps, never works!

Dirty.
Down.
Yet believing their up!
Not even worth describing anymore.

Loving an enemy becomes more than a war

At a loss in my selfish the only next step up the ladder is to turn it into a toad to go to its toad home

"My Sister's Fire"

Looking
In eyes
In voice
In manor
For her fire

It was black flame outlined in white and bright lighted purple with the smell of smoke without wood
I loved it!

Where?
When?
How?

Something simply blew it out!

The breath of that beast angered my mothers flabbergasted my fathers and sincerely confused me!

Hating that contingent blow

Seeing
Down
Drown
Depressed

But Believing the fire never faded!

Ann Wright

"Seaside at Galilee "

Scrutinizing
Not hearing
But smelling the shore-filled air
Sand
    Silky and beige with tiny pebbles mixed in scattered like His people's

Gathered with the pebbles among the sand, the people sat, stood, yet waited, listened a few milled about
A child cried
Some chit chat and laughter

Then a silence breaks with a wave at the shore
Like their hearts will at His declamation
Power filled the air
And the people changed forever
Finally encouraged

"The Word of the Lord Endures Forever"

More constant than rock
Unlike human emotion or animal instinct

Iridescent white in color
Opal made of wood in the light
Whether dim or sunny
But always shimmers
Shimmering stationary
Unlike a decorative jewel

More eternal than a first love
More everlasting than their kiss
Once capitalized with a 'K' but deteriorated, human in memory

His utterances
His shouts
His whispers even
Even His chit chat
Stands like flowing wood that never burns away

'Resounding' as they say
Lasts beyond time
For the loud silence of even his thoughts
Can create time simple to Him
Perplex to us at times

Ann Wright

"Imminent endurable earth "

Sunshine where only mud and shame once were
A ringing choir to sing the blues away
Apples—fruits
Rainbows clean rain
With a smell greater than any earthly perfumes
Fills the mind with peace

A swimmingly dreamy comfort

A new earth
Never possible of trashing

The soil!
A feel a silk to the soil producing rich with creativity
And the plants greener richer ever seen in the real
No material things
Not wanted
Not needed
New colors to flowers the greater entertainment
The flowers no smell only in the air
The product of His sacrifice and the sacrifice of his servants and followers

Our hearts deep full and clean with joy
Our minds the same with a countenance never in fall
Our skin and bones new!
Sponge and squeaky clean and strong

I wonder if we'll cook?
But I believe off the tree or vine would be perfect no need of spice or heat

And a full visualization of the truth of God mysteriously appearing when it's when

"Mom said don't play in the mud"

But we walked and played and had a ball
A ball that shouldn't be tossed, hit and never competed with
especially in the mud
 for the mud turns to grime
 and grime to trash
and trash to sick

People in their pity party competitions

Take your suffering like a cup
Like a cup to drink
And At l least walk through it
And find you blessings small and somewhere
A birds wing
A rose Thorne
Toes to balance with your feet
Clean now in the Blood

Ann Wright

"Turn it!"

Mind a tangle
That no hairbrush can cure
Thwarts, and I wonder who??
As if that can matter
Revenge left to God
I turn my cheek to the left
I turn my cheek to the right
Until I die!
The challenge feels good
A victory
A high
I can take a hit if I want
But am I addicted?
Afflicted?

With bloody cheeks
Waiting
For God's revenge
For my bloody cheeks

"Don't wait for lemons and salt"

The injustice
Still to cut
Unlike eatable fruit
But with pure blood
Spilt on the floor
Like the unfortunates
Paying for salvation with damn dollar!

The injustice
Still too fresh
Cut
Not yet rubbed with lemon and salt
Waiting...
Waiting..
No! Don't wait!
Drink lemonade
Sugar
Sugar
Sugar it up!
The injustice
He paid it with His

Ann Wright

"Rejects"

It's just a taste
Just a taste
Just a taste
    Like a rotten raspberry you digest
Only to see it was actually food
To clean?
To sicken?
To separate?
To fold into broken hands of prayer
So rise up
Rise up
Rise up
It's just a taste

" So, I'll take her with me"

A black heart— she was told and accepted as an honor
With ashes in the spider web but it was white like an angel's wings

And I'm taking her with me
Her spirit, as help

"It's tough." They told her about her black heart when they saw the kindness in her eyes
Gave it to her as protection

Everyone else seems to tell me the opposite
And it makes me wonder
If I'm anything like her

The lines on my hands are unique as hers but it's still hard to find their value on time

When the clock turns into baby giggles I'll rest easier think

And when I think, time doesn't stop as it should for me like he should, I sigh
But I'll think myself to death wondering if he loves me even when everything points to yes

So I'll take her with me
Her and her' black' heart

Ann Wright

"Peace-making "

Dragonflies
Flowers and crosses
Among the depths of my heart
Climbing to new shoes
And open doors of peace and righteousness
Where they kiss
But not on the lips

Books,
Souvenirs
And crosses
Of rain
Reigning among the simple and complex
Where they kiss but not on the lips

Phones
Dresser knobs and crosses
Inside the mind of my soul
The spirit chooses my direction
With the sinner and saint
Where they kiss
But not on the lips

"77x's"

Have you ever been forgiven?
I mean something you felt really bad about?
Something you lost slept over?
Something that turned your mind into some kind of a mousetrap tangle that no hairbrush or cheese can even cure?

I say! Have you ever been forgiven by someone other than God Himself that just surprised you?
Like it was no big deal
No sweat of their back
No exchange taken no payment expected to fee for your guilt
Have you ever been forgiven with a joke?
With a smile?
With a hug?
With a head turned away?
With a fight?

It's the dream when the reality's too much in the Blood

Have you ever had forgiveness from the meanest person you know?
Did it stick?
Did you doubt it's sincerity at first?
Or did you eat it whole in your hunger?
Fully digest
Only to eat their dirt again because their forgiveness was so out of character and so needed you ate it whole and too fast
So, you ended up choking on their dirt instead of asking for another meal??!
Have you ever needed to be forgiven so much you forgot what it felt like to be clean of your mistake?
Had you ever needed to forgive so much you walked miles in the snowy cold to do it and if you needed to give it so much did you actually need to receive it?

Has 77x's actually meant infinity to you?

Ann Wright

" Beauty and Cleanliness"

Vanity or modesty
In a time where prayer trumps reserve
When cleanliness gets in the way of your shower
Folding a line with bloody knuckles

Mascara mixed with lipstick on your nails
Bronzer mixed with fingernail polish in your hair

Scentless toothpaste
And a taintless polluted flower

-A Scarlett Gilia

"Traveling to different 'lands' "

On knees
Standing
Whispering or shouting
Through play or struggle
In tongues or English
Prayers up and out to God
As a best friend, brother or king

Flowers
Sunshine
Rainbows and rain
Psychedelic rock
Drugs
Patchouli and forgiving acceptance

Pity parties
A sad black parade
Dreary and dreamy
A pleasant nightmare if you will
With black eye makeup and color to match
The deep redness of His blood
With their broken hearts

Stationary solid and safe
Accused as sheep with a tyrannical Shepard
Never straying
Continuous in confession of tiny things
Polite and
 never rude even if necessary

Relentless fight of heavy and light faithfulness
Determination for a holy path
Narrow and discovering is never enough
A pursuit to give

Ann Wright

Victorious with the victory handing the crown to the one who gave it

Broken biscuits from the microwave when the oven's correct
Warm, dripping with honey or jam
Television and cake
Where conversation should reign

What you see is not what you feel
A land with no remedy
" can you leave?"
A land without land. Or place to land
Floor out of space
" is there time?"
No floats no skies
Clouds but no healing rain!
I can leave
Thank God I can leave!

Back home soon
A full heart with my child's face
After the winter under protection
Beautiful chipped teacups
Open doors
Loving embraces
Passion and hopeful expectations
Play and work

"Lines"

Eyes that cross
Lines that cross
Straight lines
Broken lines and Noticed lines, seen to fall between to dance up and above
To fly underneath with a mad gleam in our eyes
Popping my eyes out of head looking for who my mind once was
He pierces me back together
What I gave
What I stole- as the same
Washes me into one forgiven again and again
Lines into patterns
Good patterns
Bad patterns
Life patterns
Lines on my teeth and eyelashes
Gone with the candlelight
Lines to write and walk on
Unlike statues in more like a plaid, constant heart-filled lamp

Ann Wright

"The meek will inherit the Earth"

Kill or be killed.   In color
A common as brown saying but who wins?
I guess the dead don't care about winning or losing when pride is at its root.
Natural selection... but who would want to survive just on earth?
I have a point, but is it pointy enough to draw blood?
Maybe I'll just write about flowers
Black and white flowers

"But what other than the blood to cleanse my conscious"

Soapy blood but not in my eyes
Lemon juice for tea instead of cuts
And salt   for potatoes not wounds
It sticks
Like sap on a tree
And branches through my veins
Shampoo to cleanse my hair
77 times
It's the color found in the black and white
It's the grey when there's no excuse
It's the truthful dream when reality is too much

Ann Wright

"Duty and Responsibility"

Somewhere between duty and responsibility
She cried
Nay, shouted!
Above the mountains
A praise to God

Sometime between duty and responsibility
The flowers choked the thorns
As flowers do sometimes

Some person between duty and responsibility
She died
As people do
From the heart
A sweet repentance
As the angels sighed "finally"

"Selfish Mercy"

God's Mercy makes the black look good.
Even when it's stains the white all the way red.

We imitate His Mercy.
We only fall short into a selfish pursuit
Like a weak old joke that was never even funny
But it keeps our nose in the air

Ann Wright

"Who said a 'bum' wanted your money anyway!"

God's Mercy feels like a colorless skin raining from the sky
A color so deep in an eye it has no color
So passionate it extinguishes the pain in souls
But
Our grim acts of mercy in His shadow can barely pretend to walk
His beaming focus of Mercy
      But it's more than 'of' Mercy
His Mercy 'is' Mercy outside of a self
While our mercy only obtains mercy.

"Purity"

Dry like autumn leaves wisdom sits.... And... Waits
While creativity with it's crazy and inane genius, dances,
In fire!

But which is better?
The later free from fire but the former more free not just by feeling but also,
Wisdom creates ritual and repetition in it's safety
And creativity stands all colorful and stuff

Yet the path between is something to be seen not learned
For learning stifles the breath of the innocent
Pure in their conquests

And God, above them all
For He created and 'is' both

Ann Wright

"A Compilation"

Paper crumbles as money should
While the sound of your heart breaking was the loudest sound I've ever heard

But no bread in the rocks

The flowers choked the thrones as flowers do sometimes

With a tension thick enough for some inventive enough to bring just a butter knife

Brandished blues, matchless black and turning flowers back to their proper time when the mad-hatter seems much too sane

Tumulted-twixt-tween glowing on the triumph a tune my soul can sing

A flabbergasted night ship upon a kintly harrow

A juxtaposed meadow off melody long

I tie you around my neck
Around my finger
Around my ankle
Marrying you many more times than that

I have a point but is it pointy enough to draw blood?
"Maybe I'll just write about flowers."

"Stained green I live"

Stained green I live
In this paper house
Trying to burn it down
While the lines on my hands are as unique as hers but it's still hard to find their value on time.

Colors of cars
Colors of tile
Colors of books
    Of paper
   Of paper in books

And my face dies everyday in view of itself while the Lord is my fight not my song like most, I guess

Ann Wright

"Silent Accusations Among Lovers"

Candled hands
Handled iced glares
Where the temperature's too warm

The fiddle plays the needlepoint scissors
Cutting at the burns of what is past

Our remembering too much
As we pine for forgetfulness
Standing too close
An awkward silence too long
We kiss to forget
We kiss as a fight
Loosing our memory and betrayal in this kiss

Candled hands
Handled iced glares
Where the temperature's too warm

The fiddle plays the needlepoint scissors
Cutting at the burns of what is past

Judgements can run deep
Twisting the mind and heart
Unfray your heart with absolution
Facing the adored traitor,
Rinsing your bloody teeth in each other's eyes

Candled hands
Handled iced glares
Where the temperature's too warm
The fiddle plays the needlepoint scissors
Cutting at the burns of what is past

"dead lettuce"

Paradise in a milk carton
With holy balloons to spare
Nuts, bolts
Shining Jagged pieces of glass
Tacks
Various buttons
One-sided broken earrings
Screws, nails
Twist-ties
And used tissues

Undreaded long, black fuzzy hair
Dirt under the nails, of course
But He smells nice, like a vanilla summer sunrise

Holes in the rainbow sock hat
Tears in the dingy white t-shirt
A veritable palace on wheels

Holes at the toe of the Nike's
Worn heels
Broken and mismatched shoelaces

He does wear pants and with dignity
As if that were His only righteousness

He finds his meals
Does not beg
Although, "beggin' be no sin."

He has a disturbed smile for all He sees
But is it He disturbed by us or them by Him?

Ann Wright

God Inspired Poetry

www.ingramcontent.com/pod-product-compliance
Lightning Source LLC
Chambersburg PA
CBHW052123110526
44592CB00013B/1721